How to Spot an Otter

Written by Becca Heddle

Contents

Collins

Otters

Otters are fantastic! They can be hard to spot, but this book will help you to be an otter expert.

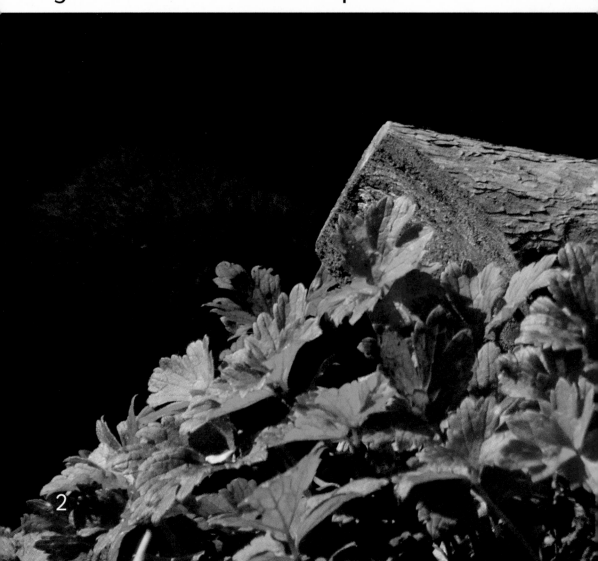

2

What do otters look like?

Otters are strong and sleek, with thick brown fur.

long, thick tail

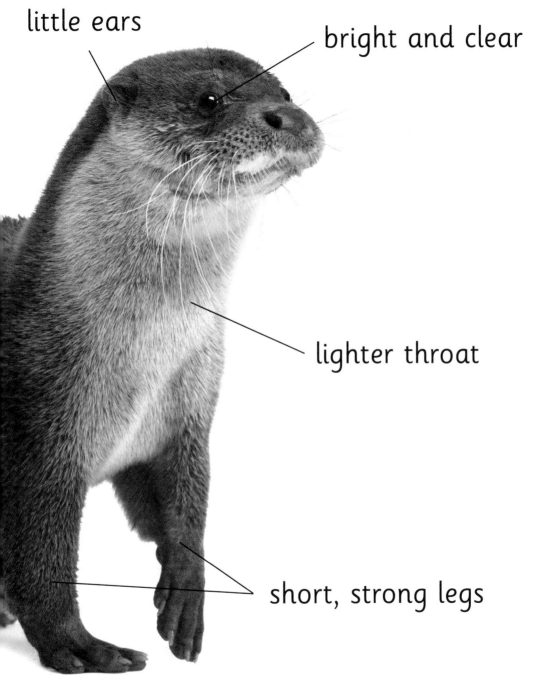

little ears

bright and clear

lighter throat

short, strong legs

Strong swimmers

A good habitat for otters is near rivers or by the coast.

They are expert swimmers.
From when they are ten weeks old,
otter pups can swim!

Smart hunters

Otters are skilful at hunting, too. They swim along rivers and hunt for fish and frogs.

They harvest crabs and shellfish from the bottom of rivers.

Otter dens

A holt is an otter den. It is often well hidden under rocks or between tree roots.

holt

Otters often creep out when it starts to get dark.

Otters must keep alert!

Otter spotting

You might spot otters in an unspoilt habitat. This river bank might be good.

Keep still to avoid frightening the otters.

Good luck!

Otter facts

Look: sleek brown fur, little ears

Skill: strong swimmers

14

Food: fish, frogs, crabs, shellfish

Den: holts

After reading

Letters and Sounds: Phase 4

Word count: 163

Focus on adjacent consonants with short vowel phonemes

Common exception words: to, of, by, be, you, they, are, like, little, when, out, what, the, do

Curriculum links: Science: Animals

National Curriculum learning objectives: Spoken language: listen and respond appropriately to adults and their peers; Reading/Word reading: apply phonic knowledge and skills as the route to decode words, read accurately by blending sounds in unfamiliar words containing GPCs that have been taught, read other words of more than one syllable that contain taught GPCs, read aloud accurately books that are consistent with their developing phonic knowledge; Reading/Comprehension: understand ... books they can already read accurately and fluently ... by drawing on what they already know or on background information and vocabulary provided by the teacher

Developing fluency

- Your child may enjoy hearing you read the book. Model reading with lots of expression.
- Now ask your child to read some of the book again, reading with expression.

Phonic practice

- Model sounding out the following word, saying each of the sounds quickly and clearly. Then blend the sounds together.

  c/l/ear
- Ask your child to say each of the sounds in the following words. How many sounds are there in each one?

  creep *(4)*   smart *(4)*   between *(6)*   throat *(4)*
- Now ask your child if they can read each of the words without sounding them out.

Extending vocabulary

- Ask your child if they can tell you the antonym (opposite) of each word below.

  dark *(light)*   good *(bad)*   under *(over)*   little *(big)*   bottom *(top)*